Simplify Your Estate

The Simple Problem Solvers

Common Sense Problem Solving Strategies for Baby Boomers... and Their Parents.
Save Time, Stress and Your Family in the Process.

By

Keith Maderer

I0476055

Part of the:

K.I.S.S.

Keeping It Simple - Single Solutions

S E R I E S

Simplify Your Estate

The Simple Problem Solvers

Common Sense Problem Solving Strategies for Baby Boomers... and Their Parents. Save Time, Stress and Your Family in the Process.

By
Keith Maderer

Part of the:
K.I.S.S.S.
Keeping It Simple - Single Solutions
S E R I E S

Websites:
KeithMaderer.com
Amazon Author Page

ISBN-13:   978-1479336326
ISBN-10:   1479336327

Special Bonus Offer

Get your
Free Video Introduction:
Listen to the Author Describe The Problem... And Solutions This Book Covers... In His Own Words
by clicking here:
http://kdmaderer.evsuite.com/ProblemSolvers

Introduction:

The Problem...

Estate planning is one of the most neglected, least favorite tasks for most people and their families. There are many reasons why. Here are some that I have witnessed over the past 30 plus years.

1. I Hate Attorneys...

2. I think it is too damn expensive.

3. It is too complicated and will take too long.

4. I am too young to worry about it.

5. I will wait until a problem arises... then I will fix it.

6. I have no idea who to appoint to handle my affairs.

7. I don't have enough assets to bother with.

8. I don't want to divulge my financial information to anyone... even my kids.

9. I don't trust my own children... much less a stranger.

10. I am afraid it will cause family problems... money always does.

11. I will wait until a friend or loved one dies, then see how **they** handle it.

12. I am afraid that if I make plans... I will die.

13. I am waiting until one of my kids brings it up.

14. I am afraid that it will upset my family to talk about it.

15. I am waiting until I, or my parents, are too old to care.

16. I Just don't care. How will it help **me** when I am gone?

17. I think it will all get taken care of after I am gone.

Pretty scary list... isn't it. If you can relate to one or more of those reasons, I hear you. Each one could be valid depending on your circumstances. But there is a solution.

The Solution...

This book provides simple solutions to these concerns. The Simple Problem Solvers are designed to help you get your affairs in order... without an attorney. No large expense...if any. No divulging your information to anyone, and no complicated legal jargon.

Just simple solutions to the most common concerns outlined above.

Sure Keith... that sounds great. But why should I trust you?

What Do I Know...

Let me share a little bit of my background. I have been a "Fee Only" financial and estate adviser for over 25 years. "Fee Only" means that my clients pay me directly for the advice I give them. I do not receive any compensation or commissions from other sources.

But I have actually been in the financial advisory business for over 35 years.

As one of the first financial advisers to complete the Certified Financial Planner (CFP) courses and pass the 6 certification exams, I became fully certified in 1990.

By purchasing this book, you and I are making an investment in each other. You pay a small price for this book... and I offer you my years of experience, wisdom and solutions to simplify your planning needs.

My clients pay hundreds, thousands, and even tens of thousands of dollars each year for my comprehensive guidance with their overall financial, retirement, income tax and estate concerns. You get one specific area of this knowledge... for less than the cost of a dinner.

This book will save you and your loved ones, thousands of dollars, headaches and arguments over the years by helping you to achieve better financial and emotional results. It will help you avoid uncomfortable, stressful situations and give you peace of mind. It is a short, focused book... without the fluff.

I have helped hundreds of clients arrange their affairs to simplify this process and minimize or eliminate probate, administration and legal costs. Let me help you do the same.

My Promise to You...

I promise that if you read this book, you can... and will, be able to find simple solutions that will help you to take care of your estate administration better, easier and with little or no expense. It doesn't have to be complicated to work. You just need to know what to do... and the best way to do it.

If, after reading this book, you do not agree... I will refund your entire cost.

Just send me an email at keith@keithmaderer.com and send a copy of your paid receipt for the book along with your name, address and phone number. I will send you a full refund.

Yes... I am that confident that these strategies will work for you.

Take Action Now...

Don't be the person who misses out on opportunities because you keep putting them off.

Be the person who sees a need... addresses it head-on... tackles the challenge, and solves the problem.

Be the person that other people see and wonder... How do they do it... I wish I had done that.

Take control of your life and enjoy the peace of mind knowing you made a great decision.

Your Challenge...

This book will challenge you to take a series of small steps that will educate and entertain you along the way.

Your challenge is to complete each chapter and finish this short book by simplifying and solving the problems that your loved ones will encounter if you are no longer there to guide them.

Don't let fear, worries or indecision hold you back. Take the lessons from each chapter and put them into action. These solutions are easy and inexpensive. You do not need a lawyer and in most cases you can handle everything privately.

I believe in you and your ability to make changes.

Don't let me, or more importantly, your loved ones... down.

Table of Contents

Why I Wrote This Book

I wrote this book, because I have been where you are. I needed to get my own life and estate plans in order. I struggled to help my parents, aunts and other family members do the same. I have seen the devastating effects that poor or improper planning can have on a family. I have experienced the pain, arguments and inter-family wars that it causes.

Believe me when I say... You do **not** want that to happen in your family.

I wrote this book because I discovered some very simple strategies that can solve these problems before they arise. Over the last 35 years, I have counseled hundreds of families that either chose to... or were forced to get their affairs in order due to medical or end of life concerns.

It really doesn't matter what has brought you to this threshold. The strategies, ideas and solutions that are outlined in this book will help you to navigate the emotions, stress and decisions that need to be made to get your life... and death in order.

I encourage you to read this book more than once. It is short... so it won't take long.

On your first pass, highlight the areas that strike you as most essential and need your attention. After you finish, go back and begin jotting down your own ideas about how you can implement these strategies to begin solving your issues and concerns.

I know that you can make it happen. I know that once you accomplish even one small part of this book, your family and life will be enhanced. I have witnessed it first hand and helped to guide many others through those same choppy waters.

The key to making it effective is to start now... hopefully before life and death offer you no choice. When you are healthy and your life is stable... your mind and emotions are always more focused and effective.

But even if you are being forced to start this process for medical reasons or the recent loss of a loved one, the exact same strategies and solutions apply. The main difference is that you, your loved ones and all those around you know that time is of the essence.

Something is wrong and the pressure is on. That stress and emotional roller coaster will make the process harder.... But it can be done.

You are one of the lucky ones. You now have a simple road map to follow which will streamline the process, reduce the time, money and stress involved... and allow you to get back to what is important... living the rest of your life to the fullest.

Who Should Read This Book

Whenever you write a book, it is important to know who your readers are. It is also important to know who **should** be reading this book, who will enjoy reading it... and who might be forced to read it.

The Perfect Candidate:

Hopefully this describes you...

The individuals that should be reading this book... aka - The Perfect Candidate... are those that are now successfully approaching retirement or have recently retired. They are married and have 2 or more children and have grandchildren or are expecting them in the future.

You have been fortunate enough to own your own home, build a nice retirement nest egg and can afford to live the lifestyle you desire. If your children need help, you feel comfortable enough that you can offer assistance.

You are realistic and know that life is at best... a day to day thing. Your general health is good, but time is taking its toll on your body, heart and mind. While you don't expect anything bad to happen, you have witnessed friends or family that suddenly died, were surprised to find a terminal illness or needed to be admitted to a nursing home.

You have a pretty good relationship with your children, their families and your friends, but there are a few things that really bother you and you have not taken the opportunity to share your thoughts and concerns because you didn't want to "Rock the Boat".

If you fall into this category... *you are the perfect candidate*.

The Need to Read... Reader:

Ok... your kids are telling you that you need to take care of this... or you need to take care of that... but you really don't want to. You just found out that something is wrong. Your heart, pancreas, lungs, prostate or mind is deteriorating. It is kind of a surprise... but not really.

You visit your doctor, but figure... hey... I'm getting older. Things happen and I have lived a good life. I don't feel like taking all those pills or watching what I eat. They want me to exercise, but I don't feel like it.

They want me to draft a will, organize my assets, appoint a power of attorney, sign a health care directive and talk about my feelings. You get defensive and angry. You tell them - "you are only after my money. I am going to spend it all before I die."

Life is for living...not cutting back on everything I enjoy. I enjoy a cold one, some chips or a doughnut every now and then... so what?

If this sounds like you, or maybe your parents... you **NEED** to read this book.
But that will be an uphill challenge that may not happen.

While it's never too late... your support and guidance will help.

The Most Probable Reader:

Unfortunately many of our "perfect candidates" and "need to read" - readers are now getting older and slightly less open-minded. Many of their children are now concerned with Mom and Dad's health, memory or care "less" attitude.

You know that they have not taken care of anything yet.

If they don't do it soon... **YOU** will be left with all the headaches.

You will be making decisions on their behalf that may or may not be what they want.

You are the most probable reader. Today we need to help our parents take the appropriate steps to get their affairs in order. It doesn't have to be hard. The simple problem solvers in this book can get the process rolling.

What I have found over the years is that when they get one thing accomplished...and it wasn't so bad... they become more interested and involved.

I suggest that you start with Chapter 2 – Simple Beneficiary Designation Solutions. Then take them to Chapter 3 – Simple Personal Instructions to Family.

If you can get them to handle these 2 items, you will have taken care of a lot of the potential problems that could arise. If they stopped right there, you will have helped them get a big chunk of their pre-planning completed.

While the rest of the topics can... and will help the family save time, money and stress, it might be all you can do for now. Take that as a victory. Provided they are in good health, you can revisit the topics next year.

Sometimes smaller projects are easier to digest. Sometimes when they see the results they have created and feel the sense of accomplishment and relief... they will be more willing to take the next step.

Give them a breather, let things settle, but be willing to listen if they want to talk. Many times that is a clue that they are ready to do more.

As with anything in life, a little humor and fun are always good. If you can add levity to the process and let them know how much you appreciate their efforts, they will be more willing to handle the necessary steps to get things done.

Document:	Date Executed:	Date Reviewed:	May Need Revisions
Health Care Directives	___/___/_____	___/___/_____	[ ] Yes [ ] No
Powers Of Attorney	___/___/_____	___/___/_____	[ ] Yes [ ] No
Last Will & Testament	___/___/_____	___/___/_____	[ ] Yes [ ] No
Trust Documents	___/___/_____	___/___/_____	[ ] Yes [ ] No

If you basic documents are in order, then it is time to move on to the Simple Problem Solvers. Each chapter will challenge you to take another step forward. Anything can be accomplished if you break it down into small tasks and take them one at a time.

Chapter 2: Simple Designation Solutions

Second Challenge:

Your next challenge is to establish proper beneficiary designations on every savings and investment account that you own. This process is much easier than it sounds. The problem for most people is they are unaware of the many ways to arrange beneficiary designation plans. You also need to make sure to avoid some common mistakes in the process.

Let's Get Started:

Estate planning can be a complicated and confusing process for many families. But the good news is... it doesn't have to be that way.

By breaking up the process into smaller and simpler actions, anyone can effectively begin estate planning.

One component of this process should be to establish designated beneficiary plans wherever they are available. In most cases this can be done with a few phone calls and filling out a form or two.

There are several factors to consider as you begin setting up your designated beneficiary plans. Here are the major items to consider as you start the process.

1. Bank, Brokerage, Retirement and Insurance Accounts:

Many people did not know that you can add beneficiaries to their bank accounts. You just need to ask your local branch office what forms are necessary and fill them out. They may call it a "payable on death" form or a Designated Beneficiary form, but whatever they call it, you want to get them in place.

Over the past decade many states have adopted a program where you can add a Designated Beneficiary plan to your brokerage accounts as well. But if you do not ask... they generally will not contact you to make these arrangements. There is no cost to add these provisions and it usually entails filling out a form or two, but the benefits will be worth the small amount of effort.

Retirement accounts like IRA's, Roth's, 401K's, 403B's, 457 plans and any other alphabet soup they can come up with... should all have specific names and beneficiaries designated on them. While you can put "as per my estate" as a beneficiary designation, this would force everything to go back through your Last Will or Trust. This defeats the purpose, benefits and original intent of the original Designation of Beneficiaries.

Insurance policies, especially life insurance, require at least one beneficiary designation. Make them specific, add contingent beneficiaries and make sure that you remember that Life Insurance proceeds paid to a beneficiary are received income tax free for reinvestment.

By establishing Beneficiary designation plans on all of these accounts and policies you will allow the institution to administer your wishes upon death instead of forcing your heirs and loved ones to go through the probate process and surrogate courts.

This is guaranteed to save time and money for your desired recipients and ensure that your wishes will be taken care of. You will also avoid any mandatory minimum waiting period requirements that could be administered on any assets that are distributed through your Last Will and Testament.

2. Joint Tenancy:

When establishing your accounts, or modifying the ownership of existing ones, consider using the joint tenancy options that are available within your state exclusively for non-retirement accounts.

If you use joint tenants with rights of survivorship (JTWROS) and one person dies, the remaining joint owner will automatically become the new owner and have immediate access to all the privileges of this account. This eliminates any time lags or need for a death certificate to continue utilizing the accounts.

It is important to make sure that you notify the institution after the death of one joint owner so they can update their records and possibly create a new account. This can be an individual account or it might be wise to add another individual (possibly an adult child) as a new joint tenant.

When joint tenancy is added with a designated beneficiary plan, these accounts will not need to be administered upon the death of either owner. This will again side step the probate and estate administration process.

But please note that joint assets do need to be included for the calculations of the deceased's estate for potential inheritance and estate tax purposes.

3. Revocable Designations:

As with most estate planning strategies, your beneficiary designations are revocable unless you designate them as irrevocable. This means they can be changed by the owner at any time... and as often as desired... in the future.

This allows for flexibility if your wishes change or one or more of your beneficiaries passes away before you. For most people, time will change some things, but I personally recommend trying to maintain fairness and equality with all of your children and other heirs.

There may be certain times when eliminating someone from your beneficiary arrangements is advisable, but make sure to modify that after the situation clears up.

Here are a few examples:

a. One of your children is going through a nasty divorce and you want to ensure that their soon-to-be ex-spouse cannot make claim to any of the assets that you intend to leave them. In this case, it might be wise to remove them as beneficiary in case something happens and inform one of their siblings to handle the distribution directly if needed.

b. One of your children's spouses is filing for bankruptcy. You may want to follow the same course of action here, otherwise the inheritance that you had planned may go directly to their creditors before they ever see a single dollar.

c. If any of your children get involved in drugs or alcoholism and are in the process of going through a rehabilitation program. It might be wise to follow the same course and wait until they are back on their feet to reinstate them as a designated beneficiary.

d. If any of your children have special medical, mental or emotional needs that require high medical costs. If they are currently entitled to federal or state aid to help pay these costs, it could jeopardize their financial benefits if they received a sizable inheritance. In this case it would be advisable to look into a special needs trust for that child to avoid the situation.

As with any revocable beneficiary designations, your ability and flexibility to make changes is something that should be used as needed. Once in place, it is usually better to leave them in place, unless one of the above situations arises.

4. Be Specific:

It is extremely important that if you are going to make the best use of these designated beneficiary plans, you need to provide very specific instructions for who gets what dollar amount or what specific percentage of each account.

Never waste the benefits of these plans to designate your "estate" as the beneficiary. By doing this you will force the assets to revert back into your estate and be subjected to administration by your Last Will and Testament, the probate and surrogate court system.

If you need more room than the forms provide because you have 7 children that you want as your primary beneficiaries and 13 grandchildren that you want to name as contingent beneficiaries, just get it typed up the way you want it and ask the institution how to make it happen.

In most instances, they will allow you to place something like the following statement on the beneficiary designation line. *"See Notarized Statement Attached"*

On this typed and formatted statement you will need to disclose a variety of information specific to your beneficiaries. You will also have to designate either a dollar amount or a percentage of the assets in that account that you want to be given to them upon your death.

The more specific you are, the better the institution will be at making sure your wishes are carried out exactly as you designated.

5. Provide Full Disclosure:

You will be required to provide adequate information about your desired beneficiaries so that the institution can properly identify them in your absence.

Make sure that you provide complete details for each beneficiary that you plan to designate in these plans. This should include name, address, relationship (son, daughter, granddaughter friend, etc.), their date of birth and tax identification or social security numbers.

If you fail to provide full disclosure of these items, it could cause unnecessary delays in setting up the plan, additional paperwork upon your death or when your beneficiaries file to receive their proceeds.

If you have any questions what the institution needs, be sure to contact them directly and ask for their specific requirements.

6. Review Regularly:

As with any financial or estate documents, it is important to keep your wishes clear and up to date. I recommend reviewing them at least every 3-5 years until you reach age 75, then every 2-3 years thereafter.

You should always review your documents and wishes shortly after any major life event and evaluate if any changes or modifications are necessary.

Major life events would include any of the following:

- Death of a family member
- Death of one of your trusted advisers
- You or a family member becomes disabled
- You or a family member is in the process of a divorce
- You or a family member are involved in any criminal or civil litigation
- You or a family member are filing for bankruptcy protection
- New children or grandchildren are born or adopted

If you experience any of these events, or when you are reviewing your documents you find there are other changes necessary, it should be very easy to change these designations by filling out a new form and submitting it directly to the institution.

Challenge and Summary:

Your Challenge: Review and establish beneficiary arrangements for each account outlined below. If you have multiple accounts of each type, make your own spreadsheet or handwritten chart to outline the following information.

Asset Account Type:	Plan Set Up	Date Beneficiary Plan Executed:	Date Last Reviewed:	Revisions Needed:
Savings Acct. #1	Yes or No	__/__/____	__/__/____	Yes or No
Savings Acct. #2	Yes or No	__/__/____	__/__/____	Yes or No
Credit Union Acct.	Yes or No	__/__/____	__/__/____	Yes or No
Brokerage Acct.	Yes or No	__/__/____	__/__/____	Yes or No
My IRA Acct.	Yes or No	__/__/____	__/__/____	Yes or No
Spouse's IRA Acct.	Yes or No	__/__/____	__/__/____	Yes or No
Company Ret. Acct.	Yes or No	__/__/____	__/__/____	Yes or No
My 401K, 403B, 457 Acct.	Yes or No	__/__/____	__/__/____	Yes or No
Spouse's 401K, 403B, 457	Yes or No	__/__/____	__/__/____	Yes or No
My Life Insurance Policy	Yes or No	__/__/____	__/__/____	Yes or No
Spouse's Life Ins. Policy	Yes or No	__/__/____	__/__/____	Yes or No
Annuity Contracts	Yes or No	__/__/____	__/__/____	Yes or No

The proper execution of a designated beneficiary plan for each bank, brokerage, IRA, company retirement, insurance or annuity contract that you own should always be the first step in any estate plan.

Generally, there are no costs to file these documents and they are readily available at most financial institutions or on their website. A few simple phone calls, a few simple forms and the regular review of these designations will simplify your estate and make the process easier for you and your loved ones.

In some instances, these plans could administer an entire estate without any probate intervention. It will take some planning to make this happen, but if you are thorough and organized... it **can** be done.

NOTE: *Even if you do get everything properly arranged with ownership's and designated beneficiary plans... it is still recommended that you have a Last will and Testament, Powers of Attorney and Health Care Directives. They may become less important, but they are important enough. They will further solidify and simplify your estate plan.*

For more information on this topic, please visit my Amazon Author Page at amazon.com/author/keithmaderer. The book entitled "Simplify Your Estate – Basic Documents Simplified" will offer inexpensive, common sense solutions to these necessary estate planning documents.

Chapter 3: Simple Instructions to Family

Third Challenge:

This challenge is one of the most helpful to your loved ones. In this chapter I will propose that you spend some time offering your experience, wisdom and instructions to your family, close friends and personal advisers. Here you will answer some of the most common questions that your loved ones will have after you are gone. Fortunately... you have the opportunity to provide these answers while you are here... and healthy.

Some Common Questions...

Who do you want to leave Mom's jewelry to?

Who should get Dad's stamp collection?

Are we going to be buried or cremated?

What priest/minister/rabbi do I want to perform my funeral service?

What funeral home do I want to have my wake at?

What food do I want served at the funeral breakfast?

Wow... isn't this going to be a FUN chapter....

Every family is unique. Parents need to let their children and loved ones know what their wishes are in the event that something happens. The reality is that many children do not have the answers to these questions before their parents pass away.

Either they have moved out of town, are too busy building their own life or they may be reluctant to face the realities of their parent's mortality. Whatever the reason, if something happens... chaos and stress can be the result.

This is exactly the reason why your **Personal Instructions to your Family** can help make their decisions and transition much less stressful. You will probably help to avoid plenty of family arguments as well.

Personal Instructions to your Family can include many things. They are not a legal document, but should be typed, signed, dated and preferably witnessed by a disinterested party or Notary Public.

They will share specific instructions about how you would like your loved ones to handle things after you are gone. Because they are not legal documents, your loved ones are under no legal obligation to follow these guidelines, but the fact that you took the time to put them in writing and have them witnessed and/or notarized will carry a strong message.

Most loved ones will do their best to honor your wishes... if they are in writing... and they are made aware of them.

Here are some specific factors to consider when preparing your instructions:

1. Burial Instructions:

Your wishes are your wishes, but if no one knows what those are, the chances of having them carried out are very slim. If you have not let your family know how, where and what you want as part of your burial, they might do something completely different.

Write down in as much detail as you can, the funeral home name, location, phone number and if you have already spoken with one of their consultants, provide their name.

Do you want a formal wake for viewing, how many hours or days, do you want to be cremated or buried, should their be a church service or just a memorial mass.

Do you want a funeral breakfast after the service, with family only or with friends, do you have a favorite restaurant where you want it held or do you want food brought over to a church meeting room.

These are the answers that you should provide for your family so they can carry out your wishes. When someone is ill and passes away, it will be an emotional and traumatic time. If you can answer their questions before they have to ask, you will allow them to address their grief and better cope with their loss.

2. Your Personal Favorites:

No... this isn't where you talk about your favorite child...

Here you want to share your thoughts about your favorite church, pastor, priest or rabbi. Your favorite bible passages, songs or hymns that you would like played or even your favorite church choir members to sing them. You can specifically mention if you would like one of your children or grandchildren to do a eulogy, share some memories or do a scripture reading.

All these items and any additional one that you can think of will help your loved ones make better and faster decisions. Your efforts here will allow them to spend more time helping the family... and less time worrying about the details.

3. Your Contacts List:

Many times, your family has expanded into different areas of the state, country or world. But it is important to make sure that they are notified of a serious illness or upon your passing. The best way to do this is to prepare a personal contacts list. It could be handwritten, typed or on a digital device, but you need to let your close family members know how to access the information and where it will be stored.

If you do not already have one handy, it would be a great item to begin compiling. In this list, make sure to highlight the people who should be notified if you become ill or upon your death, such as immediate family, close family friends, your health care agents, power of attorney and executors.

You should also make note of the names and phone numbers of those that you would like to be notified and invited to your funeral or memorial mass.

Along with that, but hopefully a much shorter list, you should also let your loved ones know of anyone that you **DO NOT** want to be notified and who are NOT invited to attend your funeral or memorial mass.

This short list of important names, phone numbers and addresses will help your spouse, children and loved ones to be better prepared and quickly handle this unpleasant but necessary task.

4. Personal Property Dispositions:

This is a fun area... strap on your seat belt... this could be a bumpy ride.

Here is where many families end up with trouble. Fighting over a parent's personal possessions has ruined more families over the years than any other estate matter. Who will get Mom's jewelry, the big screen TV, Dad's coin collection or the fine china? Unfortunately, if you do not spell out a fair and equitable system for the distribution of these items, some of your children, possibly influenced by their spouses ("the outlaws"), may feel that they are entitled to them. Others may be resentful and this is where family arguments start... and sometimes end relationships.

Here is a simple system that anyone can use to avoid this problem.

Step 1: Make a list of any specific items that you would like to go to one child or another. Place what you believe is a fair family value on those items. If your child chooses to accept the item, the fair value is deducted from their share of the estate inheritance. If they do not want this item, it can be added to the remaining inventory to be distributed in the next step.

Put this list in writing and have it witnessed or notarized by a disinterested third-party.

Step 2: Have your family arrange to meet as a group on one weekend. On the first day, have one or more of your most trusted children inventory the remaining personal property items that they believe the family should and would like to keep. With this inventory, have them all agree on a fair value for each item.

On the following day, have each of your children, starting with the oldest to youngest select one item at a time that they would like. The next round should go from the youngest to oldest and have them continue this process until there is nothing left that anyone cares to claim.

This will allow any and all of your children (and their spouses) to receive items from your estate, but there will be a fair family value attached that will be deducted from their equal share of the estate.

Over the years I have heard children and some of the outlaws say "Oh Mom wanted us to have that", when there was no cost involved. But when there is a fair value applied to that item, they tend to change their mind in lieu of a cash amount.

Those that really want to items will be more than willing to have it paid for out of their inheritance because they see its value and may have an emotional or sentimental attachment.

Step 3: Hold an estate sale for whatever is left or donate the remaining items to a local charity. Any proceeds from the estate sale should be added to the estate figures or provide each child with a donation receipt for income tax purposes.

If everyone agrees and participates, no one should have any reason to feel slighted or left out. They may even have some fun as they share memories from years gone by. In many cases it will bring them closer together as a family.

5. Personal Desires and Wishes:

In this section of your instructions you have an opportunity to leave a lasting positive impression on your loved ones. Over the years your family has grown and matured... you had a front row seat to this personal documentary.

Here is where you can share some brief highlights, ideas and wisdom that you would like them to remember you by. While children have their own views on most topics, it is always important to remember your roots... and help them remember theirs.

By sharing your beliefs, desires and wishes for how you would like your children to carry on after you are gone, it might be a nice refresher for them to remember you by. Use this letter to share any final wisdom or advice and try to finish by letting them know that you will always love them.

You might be surprised that they will listen more after you are gone... than they ever did while you were alive.

6. Personal Notes to your Children, Grandchildren, etc:

Did you ever want to share something with one of your children or grandchildren, but were afraid to mention it because they might not want to hear what you have to say. This is a great section to do just that.

Sometimes it is hard to express your feelings about certain issues to your children or grandchildren. By providing a short personal note to each of your children, grandchildren or other loved ones, it may be easier to write your feelings and clear the air after you are gone.

In many cases, these short notes could help your loved ones reflect on their actions and put their own lives on a better path. Your words may be just the motivation that they need to forgive someone, forget past problems and move forward with a positive attitude.

This posthumous feedback should always be constructive and caring. I always recommend that you start by sharing some of the items that you love and respect about them. You can then offer a couple suggestions and constructive guidance on things that you believe they could be doing better or differently. Finally finish with some motivational words and hope that they will make you proud in the future.

You always want to leave them with a caring, positive and lasting memory that they can read anytime they are feeling depressed or in need of guidance. Sometimes those few words you share with them will make a lifetime of difference... for them and their families.

Challenge and Summary:

Your Challenge: Fill in the chart below to share with your loved ones. If you have already documented the item, the date that it was updated and the location where you have the items stored. This will help your family find these items and make sure that they are honored in the event something happens to you.

Instruction Type:	Provided:	Last Updated:	Location:
Burial Instructions	Yes or No	___/___/_____	
Personal Favorites	Yes or No	___/___/_____	
Contacts List	Yes or No	___/___/_____	
Property Disposition	Yes or No	___/___/_____	
My Desires and Wishes	Yes or No	___/___/_____	
Notes To My Children	Yes or No	___/___/_____	
Notes to Grandchildren	Yes or No	___/___/_____	
Notes to Friends	Yes or No	___/___/_____	
Other: _____	Yes or No	___/___/_____	

As with all important financial and estate planning documents, it is a good idea to review them regularly and modify as needed. The same is true with these letters of instructions to your loved ones.

Surprisingly, your efforts in this section may be the most important to your family and the place where you can provide the most assistance. Spend some time now to save a lot of problems, arguments and bad feelings later on.

If you are lucky enough to have your own parents alive, share this with them and encourage them to do the same. Hopefully your positive examples will trickle down to your children... then your grandchildren... and so on.

Chapter 4: Simple Gifting Strategy

Fourth Challenge:
This chapter and challenge will be a little more involved, but can have a huge impact on the simplicity and administration of your estate after your death. There are 10 steps you will want to review and complete, but each one of them is relatively easy. After reviewing this entire chapter, take a few days to let the concepts set into your mind. You may not be ready to begin this process yet, but you will know when that time comes and have a simple road map to follow in order to do it right.

Gifting Strategies...??

Why would I want to give my savings, investments, house and retirement accounts to my children before I am gone?

What if I need those funds to live on?

What if I have to go into a nursing home?

What if I don't trust my children... or their spouses?

These are some of the many questions that I hear every time we begin discussions about lifetime gifting strategies. All of which are valid concerns and I will answer each of them in this chapter.

The systematic use of the annual gift tax exclusion can... and should be an invaluable part of any estate plan. With proper planning and some forethought, you can successfully lower or eliminate estate shrinkage from administration, death taxes and probate costs. You will also have the opportunity to give your estate plans a trial run to see how your children will react. This can be an invaluable opportunity to open the lines of communication and educate your children about your wishes at the same time.

A properly outlined and executed Lifetime Gifting program will help you pre-administer your estate and allow you to control how and when your assets are distributed.

If you have been fortunate enough to accumulate savings, investments, a house, IRA and 401K accounts over your working years... wouldn't you like to see the benefits of your hard work go directly to your children and grandchildren after you are gone?

Or would you rather have big chunks go to lawyers, the courts, your state and possibly the federal government. Hopefully your answer is... your family. If not... you can close this book and pass it on to someone else.

For the purposes of the following gifting illustrations, we will use the example of a recently retired couple in their late sixty's with three children, each of whom are now married and have two of their own children.

Simple Lifetime Gifting Strategy - Here are some factors to consider:

Step 1. Both Retired Parents are Alive and Healthy:

While both parents are alive, they can each make annual gifts in any amount up to $14,000 annually (according to the 2016 Federal Annual Gift Tax Exclusion) to each of their children

Example 1: Annual gifts to your children only (current maximum amounts)

Gifts to:	Mom's Gifts	Dad's Gifts	Totals:
Oldest child	$14,000.00	$14,000.00	**$28,000.00**
Middle child	$14,000.00	$14,000.00	**$28,000.00**
Youngest child	$14,000.00	$14,000.00	**$28,000.00**
Totals:	**$42,000.00**	**$42,000.00**	**$84,000.00**

Example 2: Gifts to your children and their spouses: (current maximum amounts)

Gifts to:	Mom's Gifts	Dad's Gifts	Totals:
Oldest child	$14,000.00	$14,000.00	**$28,000.00**
Oldest - spouse	$14,000.00	$14,000.00	**$28,000.00**
Middle child	$14,000.00	$14,000.00	**$28,000.00**
Middle - spouse	$14,000.00	$14,000.00	**$28,000.00**
Youngest child	$14,000.00	$14,000.00	**$28,000.00**
Young - spouse	$14,000.00	$14,000.00	**$28,000.00**
Totals:	**$84,000.00**	**$84,000.00**	**$168,000.00**

Hopefully you can see that this strategy can accelerate the distribution of your estate assets if you have a sizable estate. You can always gift less than the maximum each year as well. But one of the benefits that we will discuss later is the 60 month look back on gifts. The ideal objective is to gift your estate away earlier rather than later because of that 5 year look back.

Please read on to find out why you would ever want to give this much away each year.

Step 2. Trusting your Children and their Spouses:

One of the first factors to consider before executing any lifetime gifting strategy is whether or not you trust your children. To take it even further, do you trust your child's spouse (I call them the outlaws).

If you have any doubts about your children or their spouses being able to live within the parameters outlined below, you may have to alter or modify the strategy to reflect your concerns.

If any of your children are divorced, considering divorce, on a second marriage, have filed bankruptcy, are being sued or are in other civil litigation, you may have to modify or rearrange your gifting strategy.

It is important to let your children know that you are making these lifetime gifts in an effort to pre-administer your estate. Thus saving time and money, that will ultimately benefit them.

You also have to trust them not to spend the cash, property or securities that you give them unless you inform them in advance. You will need to trust that they will leave the gifts invested and untouched in case you need them for living or medical expenses later in life.

The benefit to them is that once you and your spouse pass away, they already have possession of the assets and then they can do as they please, without lawyers, courts or anyone else telling them what to do.

So how do we do that?

Step 3. Establishing Multiple Joint Accounts:

What if you need the money... after it has been gifted away?

First of all, a gift means that you are giving up all interest in the property, cash or securities that you are giving your children. If they want to go and spend it all... technically... they could.

But with this Lifetime Gifting Strategy, you need to sit down with your children before giving any gifts and discuss why you are considering it.

As outlined above the reasons are clear.

It benefits you to get the assets out of your name for nursing home, probate and estate administration purposes.

It benefits your children and grandchildren because they will ultimately get more of your estate assets with less hassles. No lawyers fee, court costs, mandatory waiting periods or misinterpretations of your wishes.

So how exactly can we set it up?

I recommend that you establish multiple joint brokerage accounts with each of your children as joint owners, with each other.

Note: This does **not** mean a joint account with you or your spouse.

Here is an example:

Brokerage Account 1: Oldest child and Middle Child – (JTWROS) Joint Tenants With Rights of Survivorship. With the oldest child's social security number for tax reporting purposes.

Brokerage Account 2: Middle child with Youngest Child – JTWROS - with the middle child's social security number for tax reporting purposes.

Brokerage Account 3: Youngest child with Oldest Child – JTWROS - with the youngest child's social security number for tax reporting purposes.

This establishes the ultimate ownership of each account... after you are gone.

The first name on each account receives the funds, removes their sibling from ownership and adds their own spouse if desired.

It also adds a contingency for the untimely death of any of your children. If one of your children dies before you, their sibling now has control of the account, not the deceased child's spouse. You can then decide how the funds in this account are to be taken care of.

They could go to the deceased child's children (or spouse). Or they could revert back to your remaining children. Other options are also possible.

Why brokerage accounts instead of savings accounts?

Brokerage accounts will allow your children to invest in a multitude of investments that can match your risk profile... or your children's if you would prefer.

Bond, equity-income and some lower risk stock mutual funds would be a conservative way to keep pace with inflation and add downside protection to a diversified and balanced portfolio.

By investing in the exact same amounts of each mutual fund on the same day for each of the 3 children's accounts, you can ensure they will all remain equal and fair as the years go by.

This will help minimize any arguing or disputes that may occur if these accounts were invested differently and one account did substantially better, or worse than the others.

Mutual funds also have a one day trading liquidity feature in the event that funds are ever needed in a hurry. Hopefully that will not be the case.

By selecting top quality no-load mutual funds and reviewing your choices quarterly, or at least annually, you should be able to make steady gains over time and allow your gifts to become even larger down the road.

Your children will pay the tax on these gains annually when they file their income tax. Some parents choose to pay for any extra tax burdens that their children incur. Others do not. The choice is yours.

Step 4. Sixty Month Look Back Period:

One of the Federal regulations that you need to keep in mind when executing a Lifetime Gifting strategy is the 60 month (5 year) look back period for gifts made to family members.

While it is fully legal to use this strategy, if either parent becomes ill or incapacitated and has to be admitted to a nursing home before the 60th month after the gifts were made, the nursing home could make claim, through the medicaid system, to the assets that were gifted and force them to revert back to the parent's account and ultimately to the nursing home.

This would only happen if you were out of money and requested to file for Medicaid or public assistance with paying for the nursing home before the 60 month period expired.

After the 60 months has passed from the date of the last gift. This becomes a non-event. All gifts are cleared and cannot be reclaimed by Medicaid through your county or state social services department.

It is advisable to keep approximately 6 months worth of nursing home costs available and un-gifted to your children. This means that if a local nursing home cost $300 per day, try to keep about $54,000 ($300/day multiplied by 180 days) available that has not been gifted previously.

This way you should not have any problem getting into a desirable nursing home and will have some time to utilize the Nursing home expense strategy that will be described later in this chapter.

Once you have the majority of your estate gifted, you can then make sure to monitor and leave the appropriate amounts in your possession.

NOTE: Each gift that is made is subject to another 60 month look back period. It is a revolving expiration of the gifts.

Example: A gift made on January 2nd, 2017 reaches its 60th month on January 3rd, 2022. A gift made on January 3rd, 2018 reaches its 60th month on January 4th, 2023... and so on.

Step 5. Upon Death of First Retired Parent:

Upon the death of either retired parent, the annual gifting maximum amounts will be reduced because only the surviving parent remains to make the gifts. Now we need to become more structured and dedicated to making these gifts because the "clock is ticking".

We no longer have the luxury of having both parents around to make gifts... and our gifting capacity is cut in half because of this.

While it is never too late to begin executing this strategy, having both parents around can make it go quicker and with less stress.

The sooner you begin using it, the sooner your 60 month look back periods will expire.

NOTE: If you start your Lifetime Gifting Strategy during December of one calendar year, you are eligible to and can give another gift ($14,000 per recipient) in January of the following calendar year. But *you cannot gift to them again until January of the next year.*

As you can see, procrastination can have a big effect on the amounts and time frame needed to properly execute your lifetime gifting strategy. So start the process now. Get in touch with your financial adviser and your children while everyone is healthy and in a good frame of mind.

Step 6. Establishing a Life Estate:

Another tool to consider within your gifting strategy is establishing a Life Estate for any real estate assets that you own. This program will allow you to transfer the deed and ownership of your home or other real estate that you occupy, such as a vacation home, to your children for as little as $1.00 depending on your state.

You can maintain the use of this property for the remainder of your life and in most cases, any senior citizen or military exemptions that you receive on your property tax bill will stay in place after the transaction.

You will need to file a new deed and in most states, this is most easily handled by a competent real estate or estate planning attorney. Life estates have become very common over the past decade and most attorneys will handle the paperwork and filing requirements for $300 on up depending on your area of the country.

Life estate transfers are classified as a gift and therefore are subject to the same 60 month look back period as all other gifts. Keep this in mind when you talk with your family in case the need arises for nursing home care or the potential sale of the house for other reasons.

NOTE: Non-owner occupied and rental properties do not qualify for life estate transfers.

Step 7. Nursing Home Expenses Strategy:

After you have executed and completed your gifting strategy, you may run into a situation where the entire 60 months has not passed before you need nursing home care. For smaller estates, you may be able to complete the process in just a few years. But larger estates may require 10 to 20 years to adequately distribute your assets.

In either case, the gifts that have surpassed their 60 month look back period are now clear and cannot be reclaimed under current rules. You do not need to consider these assets when and if you need to apply for Medicaid's help.

Only 54 months have passed... Now What?

Lets take a look at how to handle another scenario where only 54 months have passed since the gifts were made.

Should you just give up, apply for medicaid and have the entire amount of the gifts be reclaimed for nursing home expenses?

You could... but there may be a better alternative.

It may be better to gift back enough funds to cover your parent's unpaid nursing home bill for the remaining 6 months until that last 60 month look back expires.

Here is a typical scenario based on our 3 child example:

Original Gift Amt.	$168,000.00	$56,000.00	$56,000.00	$56,000.00
Month:	Nursing Home Cost:	Oldest Amt:	Middles Amt:	Youngest Amt:
55	$9,000.00	-$3,000.00	-$3,000.00	-$3,000.00
56	$9,000.00	-$3,000.00	-$3,000.00	-$3,000.00
57	$9,000.00	-$3,000.00	-$3,000.00	-$3,000.00
58	$9,000.00	-$3,000.00	-$3,000.00	-$3,000.00
59	$9,000.00	-$3,000.00	-$3,000.00	-$3,000.00
60	$9,000.00	-$3,000.00	-$3,000.00	-$3,000.00
Totals:	$54,000.00	-$18,000.00	-$18,000.00	-$18,000.00
Net Saved:	$114,000.00	$38,000.00	$38,000.00	$38,000.00

Several events, conditions and variables could affect this strategy. Here are the most important ones to consider.

- The worst case is that your parent passes away before the end of the 60th month. But there is no more need to make nursing home payments after death.

- Your parent recovers and comes home healthier. This is less likely, but does happen more today especially when the original nursing home need began as a rehabilitation from an accident, injury or surgical procedure. This also has no need for additional payments to the nursing home.

- Number of parents that gave the original gifts. Both gifting, $28,000 per child. If only 1 parent then the maximum could have been $14,000.

- Was the gift of the maximum amount. If it was less, this will make the numbers less advantageous.

- The number of children (and spouses) that received the gifts. The annual gift amount is also based on the number of children and spouses that received it. Examples: 3 children & spouses, the gift could be up to $168,000. With only 1 child and spouse, the amount may only be up to $56,000. But with 5 children and spouses, it could have been as large as $280,000.

- The larger the annual gift, the more advantageous it is to gift back and pay the nursing home bill until the 60th month expires.

- If the parents have a very low... or a very high monthly retirement income, it will affect the scenario. If the parents can afford the bill without touching the assets, you don't need to apply for Medicaid. If not, you may have to take out the entire cost from the accounts as outlined above.

- The number of months remaining before the 60 month look back expires will also affect these calculations.

Step 8. Coordinating Your Lifetime Gifting Strategy:

If you have already taken care of the basic documents as outlined in chapter 1, you will need to make sure that none of the documents that you have established conflict with your lifetime gifting strategy.

Ideally you will want to have as little as possible of your assets and estate be subjected to your will, probate, mandatory minimum waiting periods, the courts, lawyers and other administration costs. These items will only shrink the amount of your assets that will eventually be distributed to your family.

As you enter into the gifting strategy, it is always a good idea to review your other estate planning documents to see if anything needs to be changed because of your gifting program. If it does, make these changes and always keep your children, loved ones and trusted advisers aware of your actions and modifications.

Step 9. Timing Your Gifting Strategy:

When is the best time to make your gifts?

The simple answer is as soon as possible in the year. The first year that you begin making gifts, there will be a little time lag as you have to discuss your strategy with your family, establish accounts, take care of writing/depositing the checks and uniformly purchasing the appropriate investments.

But after your first gifting year, all you have to do is write your checks on January 2nd, give them to your children and their spouses (or alternative recipients), wait for them to clear and then have your child deposit the funds into the brokerage accounts for investment.

You could wait until December 31st every year, but then your 60 month look back will start and expire, as much as 12 months later each year.

Step 10. Making Out The Checks:

How do you make out the checks?

While this may sound like a simple process and a rather dumb question, you should create the proper paper trail for your gifting strategy.

Example:

If each parent is gifting to each child and their spouse... how many checks should each parent write and sign?

The answer is each parent should write and sign six checks. One for each of their children and one to each of their children's spouses. That is a total of 12 checks for this 3 children gifting strategy.

Why so formal? Why all the paperwork?

The IRS and Federal government have established the gifting rules. But if one parent made out all the checks, they could say that you gave too much in one year and then subject your gifts to gift taxes.

To avoid any questions or complications, just make out individual checks and have each parent sign them.

As for the checks from your children to deposit in the joint brokerage accounts, they can be one check as the new owner is named on the account.

Challenge and Summary:

Your Challenge: Your objective with this challenge is to fill out the chart below and make sure to review and address each of the 10 steps when establishing any lifetime gifting strategy. When you are ready to start this process, you should monitor each step and document when it is completed. This will allow you to track the timing of your gifts... as well as the 60 month look back period.

Gift Strategy Action Steps:	Reviewed:	Ready To Use:	Date Completed:
Both Parents Here/Healthy	Yes or No	Yes or No	___/___/____
Trusting Your Children/Spouses	Yes or No	Yes or No	___/___/____
Multiple Joint Accounts	Yes or No	Yes or No	___/___/____
60 Month Look Back	Yes or No	Yes or No	___/___/____
Upon Death of First Parent	Yes or No	Yes or No	___/___/____
Establish Life Estate	Yes or No	Yes or No	___/___/____
Nursing Home Needs Strategy	Yes or No	Yes or No	___/___/____
Coordinating Gifts	Yes or No	Yes or No	___/___/____
Timing Your Gift Strategy	Yes or No	Yes or No	___/___/____
Make Out Checks	Yes or No	Yes or No	___/___/____

This gifting strategy is a great way to distribute your estate assets before you die and eliminate a lot of issues that can come up after you are gone. But it does take time and cooperation from your children and family.

If you follow the rules and stay within the allowable parameters, you can save your loved ones a lot of time, money, arguments and headaches.

Chapter 5: Simple Dispute Suggestions

Fifth Challenge:
This challenge will help you to resolve problems that may arise within your family. Your goal will be to set up a written plan for handling inter-family disputes. Follow these 7 steps and you will execute a proven strategy for handling and potentially eliminating disputes before they get out of hand.

Every family has its own dynamics and while the parents are alive, they tend to mediate the arguments and personalities involved. But when they are gone, all too many families incur needless and sometimes irreparable damage to their family unit.

It could be fighting over the estate assets, arguing over administration issues or even the outside influences of an in-law. Whatever the cause, it can have a long-lasting negative impact on your family.

While every parent wishes their children would remain civil and friendly after they pass, it is one of the most common problems after a death. One of the unfortunate realities of life is that family members don't always agree or get along.

With this in mind, here are some strategies that you can use now that could help solve these issues before they arise or diffuse them before they cause irreparable damage.

Strategies to Help Solve Family Disputes:

Step 1. Pre-Planning:

Many of the problems that arise can be minimized or eliminated with some early planning by parents. Parents usually have a pretty good idea about what they envision happening when they pass away. But unfortunately, parents don't always share their vision with their children while they are healthy... or before it is too late.

If you or your own parents are in their older years, take the initiative to ask them some poignant questions. If you ask, most parents and children are more than happy to tell you their opinions. Start with basic questions and work your way into more specific areas. Their responses may surprise you, but they will definitely enlighten you.

Step 2. Communicate Early and Often:

At regular intervals as you age, take time to arrange family meetings to discuss your estate and final wishes in a casual atmosphere when there are no pending health or emotional issues to cloud one's judgment.

These are great family bonding times and can be very productive at keeping the peace. The more often your loved ones have an opportunity to share their viewpoint, the easier the process of expressing their opinions will become.

Step 3. Fairness and Equality:

If possible, try to treat all your loved ones fairly and in equal shares within your estate plans. The single biggest reason loved ones have hard feelings after the death of a parent is that they feel slighted in some way.

It could be financially related, responsibility related or even sentimentally related. If you look at your estate plans from these three standpoints and try to keep everything fair and equal, you will solve most problems before they arise.

If you are one of the few families that has a desire or need to **disinherit** a family member, make sure that you take the appropriate legal steps to properly disclose and explain your actions in the event this omission will create a family dispute. Your efforts here can be a crucial step in your estate planning and will explain to your loved one the reasons for this action.

Step 4. Coordinated Decisions:

By keeping all relevant family members in the decision loop, you can make sure that everyone is on the same page and understands what you are trying to accomplish.

If children are allowed to participate and add their opinions in an open discussion about estate plans and administration, they are much more likely to go along with the plan even if they disagree with certain aspects.

This is a great way of allowing your family to help coordinate your estate efforts and avoid disgruntled family members.

Step 5. Minimize Outlaw Influences:

In every family your children's spouses (aka - The Outlaws) are involved to some extent in the decisions that are made by each child. In most situations, these individuals are cherished members of the family and realize that it is not their position to interfere with a spouse's family arrangements.

But occasionally personalities collide and other family members may feel bullied or influenced by an outspoken outlaw. If this is the case, it is best to suggest that you involve only the natural children and exclude all "outlaws" from the direct decision-making process that will affect the rest of the family.

Step 6. Fair and Equitable Asset Distribution:

A great way to avoid hard feelings is to draft written instructions for the family about personal property distributions. First try to handle sentimental items, like family jewelry, gun collections or artwork. If you know that one of your children had a direct interest in those items, make sure that they receive them.

Be sure to have all children agree on a fair family value for each item and if they choose to keep it, that value will be deducted from their fair share of the estate totals. These special items should all be written down and have the listing notarized.

The next step should be written instructions that you ask your children to follow after you are gone. Instruct them to arrange a family weekend and on the first day, inventory the remaining personal property items.

Once itemized, have them place fair family values on all items. Then have each sibling select one item at a time beginning with the oldest to the youngest, then reverse the order to be fair. The value of the items selected should be deducted from their fair share of the estate totals.

Lastly, once the family has selected all the items they would like, have an estate sale or donate the remaining items to local charity.

If they take these steps, no one should feel slighted and everyone should have an equal chance at preserving items that they want, need or have sentimental value.

Step 7. Appoint a Dispute Resolution Person:

It is a great idea to appoint an unbiased, non-related individual to be available if needed to act as a dispute resolution person or mediator in the event that there are any disputes within the family.

Let your family know who this individual will be in advance and explain that you expect them to cooperate and adhere to any decisions that are made by this person.

Ideally this person should not be related to the family, be at least 15 to 20 years younger than you and respected by your loved ones. This person should possess a great deal of common sense and also be a good communicator.

Hopefully they will not be needed, but having them available can solve little problems before they become big ones. This person should be disclosed in your written personal instructions to the family.

If such a person exists, great. If not, do your best to find one to fit the bill.

Challenge and Summary:

Your Challenge: In order to complete this dispute resolution strategy, you need to address each of the 7 steps and help your family and close friends become part of the solution... instead of one component of the problem. Fill out the chart below and get the process in place before problems arise. Your proactive steps now could eliminate future problems.

Dispute Resolution Steps:	Reviewed:	Ready To Use:	Date Completed:
Pre-Planning the Process	Yes or No	Yes or No	___/___/_____
Communication – Early and Often	Yes or No	Yes or No	___/___/_____
Fairness and Equality	Yes or No	Yes or No	___/___/_____
Coordinated Decisions	Yes or No	Yes or No	___/___/_____
Minimize Outlaw Influences	Yes or No	Yes or No	___/___/_____
Fair and Equitable Distribution	Yes or No	Yes or No	___/___/_____
Dispute Resolution Person	Yes or No	Yes or No	___/___/_____

Grief causes emotions to run high and this can make people respond irrationally. If you prepare your loved ones early and keep the lines of communication open, you will have great opportunity to avoid family disputes entirely.

If your family is geographically disbursed, you can always arrange a meeting around the holidays or other family gatherings. It is usually best to start the process with your own children first and add their spouses (the in-laws) to the mix later... if necessary.

If you follow all or even some of these methods, you are guaranteed to provide a much smoother estate transition than if these topics were never discussed until your passing.

Have fun with it and try to keep things informative and concise. Preparing a one page written "family agenda" that summarizes your ideas will keep things moving forward.

Remember to always leave a spot at the end for questions and answers. These discussions could help shape your future plans and additional meetings.

One of the most common regrets that individuals who are terminally ill express is that they never took the time to share their true wishes, feelings and ideas with their loved ones.

This process will allow you to do that and solve one of the biggest problems every family faces upon your death.

Chapter 6: Bonus Strategies and Solutions

Sixth Challenge:

The sixth and final challenge is to take a look at the following 8 Bonus Items and see how they might fit within your plans. Each of them is based on real life situations that I have encountered over the years. If they sound relevant to your own personal situation, add them to your plans and be sure to update your loved ones with your decision.

Bonus 1: Top Ten Bucket List Items:

Every day we are alive is a blessing... but if we don't keep challenging ourselves on a regular basis, life can get boring, routine, and mundane. What fun is that?

My challenge to you is to make a short list of the top 10 things that you would like to do before you leave this earth. Take those top 10 things and prioritize them based on your ability and desire to accomplish them.

Then start stretching your comfort zone. Take your top priority item and make it a reality. If its riding a hot air balloon, skydiving or zip-lining... ask your family to join you and just do it. Who knows... it could be on **their** bucket list as well.

If its writing a book... (that used to be on m bucket list) then sit down, give it a title and start making an outline. There are plenty of books about writing books... get one and get going. One of my favorites is **The Miracle Morning for Writers** by Steve Scott, Hal Elrod and Honoree Corder. https://amzn.com/B01FWGH4GO

Once you accomplish your top priority bucket list item... cross it off the list and start working on number 2.

You will be surprised how rewarding this can be. If you include your family, friends and others, it will be even more fun.

So start stretching that comfort zone and make the rest of your life an adventure.

Bonus 2: Don't Forget Pets:

If you have or have ever had a pet, you know how strong the bond can be with their owners. But often they are left out of the estate planning strategies and need to be put up for adoption.

Illnesses and death of an owner are just as traumatic on a family pet as they are on the other family members. Remember the feelings that you had when your pet passed away or had to be put to sleep. This is a sad and emotional moment... and our pets do react similarly to humans.

If you have a family pet, don't forget to make arrangements for who will take care of them if you are gone. In many cases this can be added to your Last Will and/or your Instructions to Family. You can also allocate a specific amount of money that can be left for the person who will receive your pet for food, shelter and medical care after you are gone.

While this may sound crazy to those who have never had a pet as apart of their family... I am a firm believer and proponent of this strategy.

Pets are loved ones. They are living, breathing creatures with feelings and emotions. They deserve to be considered as part of our estate plans. They deserve to be cared for and loved by another after we are gone. Don't forget to add them to your wishes.

Bonus 3: Pre-Plan Funeral Arrangements:

Your funeral arrangements can be one of the toughest things that your family will have to complete upon your death.

First they are already in a vulnerable and emotional state because of their loss.

Second, the funeral process is set up to benefit the funeral home and their sales people. Because of your emotional state, they prey on your guilt and feelings of loss. Wouldn't you want your loved one to be buried in the best? Many families end up spending significantly more for a funeral than you would want them to... because of this.

The Solution: Prepay, pre-plan and pre-select your funeral arrangements. You are the best person to decide what type of funeral you want.

Do you want a fancy casket, or a wooden box for your burial?

A diamond studded urn or a Guinness beer bottle for your ashes?

A 3 day funeral with a wake and church mass or a simple private family get together?

A small family funeral breakfast or invite everyone who attends?

There is no one better than you... to decide what you want it to look like. So take the initiative and set up years in advance. You can pay for it in advance with the funeral director of your choice and they place your payment in an escrow account that will earn interest and will be used to pay for your funeral when that day eventually comes.

This will take a great burden off your spouse and children as most of the hard decisions will be made by you, while you are healthy and not in an overly emotional state. You can pre-select all the items and keep the costs in the range that you feel is appropriate.

In most situations, you will be much more frugal and conservative with the arrangements than your loved ones will be "persuaded" to be after you are gone.

This allows them to focus on grieving and fellowship with those that are in attendance and sharing their fond, humorous, fun stories and memories about you.

For more information about this process, here is the link to a great article by ElderLaw Answers - Pre-Paid Funeral Plans: Buyer Beware - http://www.elderlawanswers.com/pre-paid-funeral-plans-buyer-beware-1098# and another link to the Federal Trade Commission (FTC) website – Shopping for Funeral Services – https://www.consumer.ftc.gov/articles/0070-shopping-funeral-services.

Just make sure that you do your research and compare costs at a minimum of two funeral directors before making your final decision.

Bonus 4: Give it a Trial Run... Die Twice:

This may sound crazy, but it can be a great way to prepare your family for what will happen and how they will feel when it does. Obviously this is just and exercise, but after you have mapped out your plans, established your documents and written a brief set of personal instructions, do a trial run.

Hopefully you will have had several family meetings to discuss your ideas, and theirs, over recent months and years. This will make it easier to let them know that you are going to have them do a test run to see what they remember and if there are any things that everyone believes would need to be modified, added or deleted.

You start by having them all sit down, preferably have a small healthy meal and then let them know that after dinner, you will leave the room which will symbolize your death. You can go for a walk, head off to the other side of the house and watch television, or whatever. You just need to disappear for a minimum of 60 minutes, longer if they need more time.

During this time they are asked to begin preparing as though you had just passed away. Have one of them act as a recording secretary to write down all the steps that they are taking and where they run into any obstacles or confusion.

They should know where to look for all documents, funeral and personal instructions, contact lists and anything else that will help them navigate through the process.

The greatest part about this exercise is that you are not deceased. They will have less pressure, emotions and urgency now because they know this is just an exercise. But it will most likely present few obstacles, challenges and opportunities for them and yourself to make adjustments that will make the actual event of your death much more efficient and help simplify the process.

During this exercise, everyone will find out who is the most emotional, most capable and most effective leader. This may be an eye-opener for some... or it could just be a great confirmation of your choices and decisions.

Either way, this simple process should be fun and educational.

After the exercise, ask them all for feedback and offer your own. Ask them if there is anything else that they would like you to do to make the process easier. Take notes and decide if their suggestions are valid and actionable. If they are, make the changes and be sure to let them all know that you took their advice and modified your plans accordingly.

By letting them know that you valued their opinions, they now feel more connected to the process and will be better prepared to participate when death occurs. More importantly, this open communication and cooperation will probably trickle down to their family when the timing is appropriate.

That would be a great family tradition.

Bonus 5: Last Letter, Recording or Video:

Over the years I have encouraged and witnessed many people that are terminally ill. One thing that many of them regret is not telling their loved ones something important. It might have been something that they were proud of, something they are ashamed of or something that they wish they would have done or said.

Because some people are just uncomfortable with confrontation or emotional sharing, I encourage them to write it down in a letter, record it to an audio CD or capture it on a short video.

These final words, thoughts and sentiments will be a lasting memory for your loved ones and may help dramatically in the healing process.

Be sure to always end on a positive note and let them know that you love them and will always be looking out for them from above.

You can place these thoughts in a safe place and make sure they are informed that they exist and where they can find them.

Bonus 6: Passwords and Digital Life:

What about my passwords... ???

Who will know how to access my online accounts. From banking, brokerage, blogs and email accounts to Facebook, Twitter, YouTube and LinkedIn.

If you have had any digital life, you will need to make sure that your heirs can access those accounts to either close them out... or continue your work.

If you have an online presence, it is advisable to make sure that you have a written paper copy of your passwords in a safe place. I recommend that you have a typed sheet or a Password Organizer with each online account that you regularly use along with its login ID and password.

Here are a couple links to Free Printable PDF - Password Organizers:

https://www.pinterest.com/pin/62276407323750203/

http://hellocuteness.com/2013/01/free-printable-whats-my-login-password-tracker/

I am sure you can create your own with a word processor or spreadsheet or find plenty of other free downloads with a quick search on google for –

Free PDF Password Organizers.

This area is becoming a much larger issue as many, many more senior citizens have jumped into the digital age. Help your family now by documenting your digital records.

Bonus 7: End of Life Decisions:

DNR... Hospice... Palliative... End of Life care?

While these items are usually the last decisions that have to be made, a little forethought can make them substantially easier on your entire family.

As we age, we encounter family and friends that are already confronted with these issues. Take an interest in their situations and offer to help with any research or obtaining information on their behalf.

It is always easier to digest this type of planning when it is not directly related to yourself. Use this opportunity to learn more about the end of life support systems that are available in your area. This hands-on research will help make your own decisions much easier to make when the time comes.

Bonus 8: Six Things To Say... Before You Go:

The following six phrases can have a tremendous impact on the lives of those that hear these words from you. While I suggest that you share them long before you need to... like now. For many people, it is hard to swallow your pride and they wait until a terminal illness or severe accident brings them to the edge of death.

Read these phrases to yourself and then make a list of who you would like to, or should, say them to. Then take that list, prioritize it and start the process now. You will be pleasantly surprised by the reactions of the recipients and how much better you will feel. It may even repair or rejuvenate a love or friendship that you thought was gone for good.

I'm Sorry...

I Forgive You...

Thank you...

I Love you...

It's OK and I am Ready to Die...

Goodbye...

Challenge and Summary:

Your Challenge: As you review the 8 Bonus Items we just covered, fill out the following chart and let your family know that you have considered these items. If you have executed any of them, let them know where they can find the details and items. This will help them locate and share your actions as needed.

Bonus Strategy	Reviewed:	I Will Use:	Date Completed:	Location:
Top 10 Bucket List	Yes or No	Yes or No	___/___/_____	
Don't Forget Pets	Yes or No	Yes or No	___/___/_____	
Pre-Plan Funeral	Yes or No	Yes or No	___/___/_____	
Trial Run - Death	Yes or No	Yes or No	___/___/_____	
Last Letter or Video	Yes or No	Yes or No	___/___/_____	
Passwords - Digital Life	Yes or No	Yes or No	___/___/_____	
End of Life Decisions	Yes or No	Yes or No	___/___/_____	
Six Things To Say	Yes or No	Yes or No	___/___/_____	

I hope you will take the ideas, strategies and information in this section and make your current life and the lives of your loved ones better. It is the small details that make us unique.

These same small details will help your family through these emotional and stressful times. Communicate your ideas, wishes and thoughts early and often.

It will be worth the effort.

Chapter 7: Simple Action Plan and Conclusion

If you have come this far, you are now ready to begin taking control of your life and estate plans. You are probably concerned that there are a lot of things to get done. Yes... there are. But if you take them in small steps as outlined in the action plan below, you will have your house in order in a relatively short time.

Each one of the following steps will become a small victory in itself.

Each step will begin helping you and your family to resolve the estate issues that may have been overlooked or ignored.

Each step will save you and your family time, money, headaches and possible arguments down the road.

Each step will give you peace of mind knowing that something good can now happen... if something unexpected or bad happens to you.

So lets start the process and check them off the list when they are completed.

Your Simple Action Plan:

Step 1:

Scan the Estate Planning overview in Chapter 1. If you haven't drafted the basic documents yet, you might want to order that book now so you can get those in place at the least possible cost and have them ready to execute after you finish the steps in this book.

Step 2:

Begin checking your existing beneficiary designations and establishing new ones as outlined in Chapter 2. this is a huge step and it is so simple. You make a few phone calls, fill out a few forms and get them back to the institution. There is generally no cost other than postage and maybe a few photocopies.

You may be able to administer your entire estate just from the strategies in this section. That doesn't mean that you should quit there. The remaining steps will help you, your surviving spouse, children and loved ones even more in a multitude of other areas.

Step 3:

Strongly consider all the items mentioned in the Personal Instructions to Your Family - Chapter 3. You may not need to sit down and write more than a handful of notes and letters to get this section resolved, but if you need more... take the time to do them.

These tend to be some of the most beneficial moments that you will have when writing them, and they are guaranteed to be some of the best memories and keepsakes that you can leave your loved ones.

What I have found for many individuals is that just the thought process and writing of these instructions, can be a great healer and a cathartic revelation in itself. Don't pass up this opportunity to live a happier life and provide your family with a lasting memory.

Step 4:

Begin working on Chapter 4's lifetime gifting strategy. This one will take only a couple of hours each year to get started, but will need to be a consistent annual New Years practice if you want to receive the full benefits of the strategy.

This program will provide a welcome solution to the many nightmares you hear about after the death of a loved one. The more you can distribute your estate before you go, the easier everything else becomes after you are gone.

Step 5:

Some of you may say, my family will never fight over my estate or my assets. Those were the same famous last words of many people and celebrities that have had their assets tied up in court battles for years.

The unfortunate reality is that sometimes people hold everything in until the death of their parents. Then it all explodes like a volcano that was dormant for years.

The dispute resolution strategies in Chapter 5 are very quick and easy to set up. If your family never needs them... great! But if they do... you and they will be glad they were established.

Don't leave this item to chance. Be proactive and open about the possibilities. In many cases, just having the process established in advance will make the potential disputes disappear before they ever happen.

Step 6:

Take the bonus strategies and solutions from Chapter 6 and utilize them to enhance the programs that you have already completed. While none of them are mandatory, each of them will make a potential problem... disappear.

As you review these items, pick and choose the ones that hit home with you and your spouse. Take those and act upon them.

Then go back and look at them again. Are there any that would make the lives of your children or other family members better? If so, sit down with those family members and ask for input, then check it off the list.

Step 7:

Congratulate yourself and your family. You have completed the simplest, least expensive and potentially the most effective steps to ensure that your estate gets handled better than many formal estate plans can do.

But even though these steps can handle many of your estate planning concerns, there are some that only the formal documents can address. Be sure to look at my **Amazon Author Page** – **http://amazon.com/author/keithmaderer** - and consider getting those in place as well.

The cost and time commitment are minimal... and the potential headaches they can save are huge.

Conclusion:

I have seen the strife and struggles that loved ones go through upon the death of a parent and know the importance of trying to keep a family in tact after it happens.

Emotions run high and feelings can be hurt with a simple comment. Everyone is on edge and it is very common to have disagreements that turn into all out wars.

You can make sure this does NOT happen in your family by taking the preemptive steps that are outlined in this book.

Don't allow your family to disintegrate after you are gone. That would be such a waste of your lifetime... and theirs.

Open Offer to You:

If you have any suggestions for additional strategies or solutions that have worked for your family, or would just like to talk, I can be reached by email at: keith@keithmaderer.com. Leave me a message and I will do my best to respond to all requests.

About the Author

Keith Maderer is an author, a dynamic and humorous speaker, an entrepreneur and a 30+ year veteran of the financial services industry. He completed the Certified Financial Planner (CFP) program in 1990 and has been a Fee-Only Registered Investment Adviser operating in Orchard Park, NY which is a suburb in the Buffalo/Niagara Falls region - since 1989. He works with individuals, pension plans and trusts to help them make simpler and better financial decisions.

He has been married to his high school sweetheart (Lori) for over 30 years (I hear she is up for sainthood) and has 5 adult children and 1 grandchild. He has been active in many local non-profit organizations and has served as a coach, League Commissioner and President of the Orchard Park Little League baseball program. He was the co-founder, President and team coach of the Orchard Park Youth Basketball Association and was the founder and managing director of the Maderer Foundation.

He actively volunteers in the District 65 Toastmasters International organization where he has served as President of both the Clarence Toastmasters and Larkin Leaders Toastmaster groups. He has achieved their highest designation of excellence in public speaking and leadership – the DTM (Distinguished Toastmaster Award) after only 4 years in the program.

He was the recipient of the Toastmaster's District 65 – Division A – Club President of the Year award in 2014 and the District 65 - Area Governor of the Year award in 2015. He was the first runner up in the District 65 International Speech Contest in 2016 and loves sharing stories, anecdotes and messages that help motivate and inspire others to achieve their own success.

His hobbies include Reading, Biking, Hiking, Photography, Golf, Disc Golf and playing with his grandchildren.

For more information about Keith Maderer or to sign up for his **VIP email list**, please visit his website at KeithMaderer.com

When you sign up for the **VIP email list**, you will receive first notification of future book launches and special offers exclusively for insiders. These may include, but may not be limited to:

1. Limited time - free download offers for Keith's future books
2. Limited time - free download offers for other publications that we have negotiated.
3. First look previews and sample chapters of Keith's upcoming books
4. First look at articles and blog posts that Keith publishes.

Other Books By Keith Maderer

Please check out my other print and ebooks on **Amazon.com**, my Audio-books on **Audible.com** and online courses on **Udemy.com**. (coming soon)

Life Insurance... Who Needs It?
What Life Insurance Agents may not tell you... but YOU need to know... Before you buy
http://amazon.com/author/keithmaderer

Simplify Your Estate – The Simple Problem Solvers
Common Sense Problem Solving Strategies for Baby Boomers... and their parents
http://amazon.com/author/keithmaderer

How Much House... Can I Really Afford?
Practical Tips to Avoid becoming "House Poor"
https://www.amazon.com/dp/B01FQ8RL0W

Simplify Your Estate – Basic Documents
Common Sense Estate Planning Solutions – Getting the Basic Documents Setup Correctly and Inexpensively
http://www.amazon.com/dp/B009F4LXE4

How To Get Your College Education... For Less
Help Design Your Own Financial Aid Package – Multiple ways to Cut Your College Costs
http://www.amazon.com/dp/1453820531

Your Opinion Matters

You are the only one that can let me know if this book is helping you with your decisions and planning efforts. I truly appreciate that you decided to purchase, read and act upon this information.

I have one small request. If you would kindly write a short positive review for this book on Amazon.com, it will help me to make changes, answer additional questions and offer further valuable solutions on this and other topics.

Please let me know specifically what your liked most, what you thought could use some improvements, as well as any other items you found useful.

If you click the link below it will take you to Amazon where you can sign in and share your thoughts about this book. Thank you for your effort on my behalf. I truly appreciate your time and effort.

Click Here to Review: **Simplify Your Estate – Simple Problem Solvers**

Then sign in to your Amazon account, select the book to review, write and post your review.

Your Review could be the deciding factor to help someone decide to purchase this book and avoid some costly mistakes. Please share your thoughts.

Thank You.

Please Share on Social Media

Please feel free to share this book with friends, family and coworkers on Facebook, Twitter, Pinterest, Google+ or LinkedIn. Only by your word of mouth can indie authors like myself build a following that can help shape future projects and help others succeed and avoid these mistakes.

Just Copy and Paste this Text and Link below – **Thank you**

I just read this book – Great information to help solve the most common estate problems.   http://amazon.com/author/keithmaderer

Facebook Share - Click Here

Twitter Share – Click Here

Pinterest Share – Click Here

Google+ Share – Click Here

LinkedIn Share – Click Here

www.ingramcontent.com/pod-product-compliance
Lightning Source LLC
Chambersburg PA
CBHW030017190526
45157CB00016B/3109